Other works by JV Connors

Love Catalogue, Book 1:
Poems for 101 Varieties of Love

Love Catalogue, Book 2
Poems for 97 More Varieties of Love

Poems on the Road to Love

Obstacles, Passages, Healing & Magic

by JV Connors, Ph.D.
with photographs by Kathleen Connors

Poems on the Road to Love:
Obstacles, Passages, Healing & Magic
by JV Connors, Ph.D.
with photographs by Kathleen Connors

2nd Edition c
Copyright, 2020
ISBN# 978-1-7352460-0-0
Interpersonal Peace Center
Silver City, NM
self-published through Amazon
looking for an agent / publisher

Dedicated to my grandmother, Marguerite Mary Bennett, nee Finn, who nourished me during my childhood with devotion, ice cream, Irish melodies and lots of love.

This book is also dedicated to Boots Doyle, Robert Whelan, Billy Ray Browning, Jesse M. Young and Andrew Sieff for their kindness and invaluable support earlier in my life.
I pray someday to prove equal to the examples these good people set for me.

Contents

List of Photographs

Chapter 1: Obstacles & Illusions

1. Illusions
2. Relationship Fantasy
3. Comfort
4. Autopilot
5. Self-Deception
6. Conforming
7. Outsiders

Chapter 2: Passions

8. Emotional Arousal
9. Animal Nature
10. Male & Female Bondage
11. Social Power
12. Sadness
13. Anger
14. Regression
15. Uncentered

Chapter 3: Struggles

16. Quiet
17. Chaos
18. Dance Partner
19. Tangles of Relationship
20. Chain of Causality
21. Relationship Insanity

22. Gender Mazes

23. The Two Faces of Sex

24. Masculine Power

25. Emotional Numbing

26. Sickness

27. Aging

28. God Bless Us When We Fail

Chapter 4: Failures

29. Walls

30. Parent-Child Burdens

31. Crushed

32. Layers of Grief

33. Old & Bitter

34. Sad & Lonely

35. Disappearing Women

36. Racial Divisions

37. Poverty

38. To Our Soldiers

39. Cruelty

40. Hate Rising

41. Old Friend

42. Letter to Our Children's Children's Children

Chapter 5: Lightening Up

43. Lightening Up

44. Laughter

45. The Offensive Idiot Test

46. Eluding Drama's Capture

47. Accident

48. Prayer to Shut Up

Chapter 6: Healing

    49. Solitude

    50. Space

    51. Anchors

    52. Friends

    53. Apology

    54. Forgiveness

    55. To Those Left Behind

    56. Misunderstanding - Understanding

    57. Discernment

    58. Harsh Transition

    59. In the Middle of Catastrophe

    60. Love Will Save Us

    61. A Little Wisdom

    62. Prayer for Balance

Chapter 7: Opening

    63. Changing

    64. Vulnerability

    65. Finding Answers

    66. Being Single

    67. Truth

    68. Consciousness

    69. In 10,000 Years

    70. Prayer for the Invisible

Chapter 8: Being

    71. The Road Continues

    72. Family Love Patterns

    73. Compassion

    74. Kindness

    75. Gratitude

76. Presence

Chapter 9: Magic

   77. Peace
   78. Beauty
   79. Precious
   80. This Moment
   81. We

Background Notes

Acknowledgments

Quote References

About the Author / Photographer

List of Photographs
All photographs by Kathleen Connors
© 2020

Cover: Road to within
Frontispiece: Morning after the storm

1. Charles in the garden
2. Ruin doorways
3. Deer hiding after the snow fall
4. Wall-tree caress
5. Back alley after the rain
6. The road unknown
7. Dark storm - New Mexico
8. The old rock wall
9. Remembrance
10. New Mexico clouds
11. Pilgrim at Santuario de Chimayo
12. Chapel of San Pedro, Tucson, Arizona
13. First crocus of spring
14. Horses after the snow fall
15. Through the fog
16. Beautiful weed
17. Summer blooms
18. Road to within (crop)

Chapter 1: Obstacles & Illusions

Love is merely a madness and, I tell you,
deserves as well a dark house
and a whip as madmen do, and the reason
why they are not so punished and cured
is that the lunacy is so ordinary
that the whippers are in love, too.

William Shakespeare (Rosalind speaking),
As You Like It (1623)

Illusions

Shape, color and distort
our perceptions every moment
clouding our minds to the present
and the people around us.

To avoid the torment of uncertainty
we spin fantasy worlds of meaning
with stories of bliss and misery
to fit family and friends around.

We may believe that life is a battle
and scan every crowd for opponents.

We may believe that tragedy haunts us
and shape every action to defend
against loss.

When we cling to our movie
and its predetermined plot
we stumble around in a thick fog
that obscures everything but ghosts
and get lost.

We cannot listen beyond our agenda
to hear those who love us —
their struggles
their worldview
their inner journey
their disappointments
so we break their hearts.

We complain others have so much power over us
but blame only strengthens the fever
that keeps us chasing phantoms

and losing people.

If we could see our loved ones
without squeezing them into roles
we could make room for more love
in our story.

Real freedom and real love
never happen in a fantasy.

Relationship Fantasy

During our time with each other
we build huge cities in the air
elaborate projections
of light and dark

With filmy images
that look real when illuminated
by expectation and passion.

Thousands of these flags hang between us
flapping noisily
drowning out our voices,
though many of us come together
for a time.

That love can find any of us
in these rumbling, littered streets
is a miracle.

How amazing to behold
the kindness and protection
that can still link us
when our eyes meet.

Comfort

We are always seeking comfort
yearning for its ease and succor
wondering why it eludes us
so often.

A welcoming lover,
friend or parent,
a nourishing meal,
a soft bed or reading chair
in a warm dwelling.

Will comfort heal us?
Bring us peace?
Calm our nerves?

Or will it addict us?
Lure us away from the vibrant life?

How strong the urge is
to curl up in a cozy nest
avoiding stress and strain

Immersed in pleasant safety
instead of thinking
about nagging details.

Hiding from life
to block out its prickly, messy beauty.

Autopilot

When we must react quickly
we follow the ruts in our brains
and choose the most familiar
most primitive, responses —

You're wrong!
It's not my fault!
Get out!

Early, intense experiences
are encoded in our neural paths
determining the choice points we see
and the solutions we pick.

So our most terrible memories
may become the base for drama cycles
that pull us into the same old dance
with tired steps and useless turns
that push us into aversion and fear.

Until we will our behavior to change,
like turning an iron post
heaving and pushing,
until it points in another direction.

Self-Deception

We all think we are good guys
even violent bullies
and leaders who order massacres.

Our minds see only what justifies
our ego's wishes
and we remain the hero
no matter how we treat others
or disrespect ourselves.

Dozens of mental distortions
excuse the disturbances we cause
and confirm our most idiotic desires.

Overconfidence is our biggest flaw
denying all mistakes
blocking out our unkindness, lack of tact
and the harm we do,
while faulting others
for any nasty consequences.

Conforming

Conformers will pay any price
for connection
molding ourselves to others' expectations
and empty trends.

Following our friends and lovers
to whatever they push —
noisy bars
expensive restaurants
obnoxious gatherings
overpriced vacations
underpaid work
degrading sex

For the privilege of their company
the fantasy of belonging.

The pain of separation is intolerable
so we'll do anything to avoid it,
but if we must be exiled
sometimes the anguish
will help to awaken us.

Outsiders

Feel awkward with people
can't play social games
tense up, panic,
How can we escape?

Outsiders live the trial of otherness
the lone wolf
no place in the hierarchy
no value to social climbers.

We long for acceptance
or mere friendliness,
yet mistrust it.

We may strive to fit in
mimic the moves, smile,
but never quite make it
to the comfort of normality.

Some outsiders refuse to try
because we cannot pay the price —
we can't follow the rules,
we value freedom
to choose our own ways
and talk of different things ...

So we become a strange object
that challenges conformers deeply
bringing curious stares, gossip.

Our allies shift with the winds,
though attracted to our fire
and the titillation of difference,
they don't feel the rooting pull of our vision

so they often disappear.

The dream of acceptance
torments and eludes outsiders
as we endure the hard path of otherness
that is written on our bones.

Chapter 2: Passions

Love shook my heart
Like the wind on the mountain
Troubling the oak trees.

Sappho (630-570 BC)

Emotional Arousal

When our feelings get out of control
crazy hormones poison us
and make us unable to think

So we shriek and roar
assaulting everyone
with childish harangues.

In our frenzy
we loudly announce
the stupidest parts of our character.

Every tantrum regresses our minds
and damages our heart
while taking a heavy toll
on those who share our company.

When emotions become intensely aroused,
we throw away our self-control
and rage at our companions
abusing their open softness.

Over time, these fits
bruise and scar every tender heart
break down caring
and drag everyone's good
through the dirt.

Animal Nature

Our connections with people
are grounded in animal nature

Bringing power dynamics
gut responses
instinctive pushes and pulls
and glancing exchanges.

Despite our best intentions and commitments
something lurks inside,
worrying, *Are you a threat?*

So our wild defenses
push for power over others
snarling at our pack mates
to dominate and manipulate them.

Our loving wishes are often subdued
by that survival drive
as we badger others to feed our hungers
despite their feelings.

Animal nature then becomes our master
and we smile when others give in,
Yeah.

Male & Female Bondage

Illusions of bliss and enemies
have imprinted male and female natures
for fifty thousand years —
creating separate reality bubbles
with diverse wants and ways of seeing.

Most of us remain confined
in these two gender boxes
to manage reality scenarios
for mating, work, and socializing.

We pattern-bound females and males
can share fluids and sensations
but our messages must pass through
thousands of light years in space —
what we hear is like underwater echoes
so we read each other's expressions
and guess at the message.

We watch how each other conforms
to the characters in bad soap operas
and jump into the masks and costumes provided
so we can play the part and win the prize
if we do it well and the judges are kind.

If we fail to please
the penalty can be humiliation
booed off the stage into the cold lonely.

Being a successful member
of the gender binary club
gives us many privileges

as we smile and try to fit in,
but it is a world of profound separation
that prevents us so often
from knowing who we really are.

Social Power

Struggle for power is the oldest dynamic
a primary human blueprint
that has shaped our DNA —

Compete for survival
take everything we can
and push everyone else behind.

Better be top dog
meaner than the rest
fighting without mercy
to live another day.

We still live by this
and battle for power every moment
pushing up
or being pushed down
in our relationships
being reminded of our place
in tiny and traumatic ways.

Social power guides every interaction —
every work relationship
every community connection
every mother, father, lover, friend
filters their caring
through the pressures of power and control.

In this predatory world of ours
there can be no other way
until we are brought to our knees
ten thousand times
to find that human connections work better
with some degree of equality.

Sadness

Crawls through our flesh
and settles in our blood
feeding us
slow down, reconsider
and *worry.*

Sadness feels every wrongness
every insult
every loss
and wants to examine their wounds
to understand their many messages
about our places with each other
(obsessing on hurt).

Sometimes sadness gets stuck
unable to let go of our living juice
pushing to control us.

It's quite a battle to get free —
there are many triggers that pull back,
saying,
Life is too painful,
I am so damaged,
It is too much to bear...

Many of sadness's slaves surround us
but we must not judge them;
just acknowledge their sorrows
and try not to feed the monster.

We could push away the burdens of sadness
refuse its control over our bodies and minds

wipe it off our faces and bellies
and walk away from it
envisioning our freedom
glowing inside.

Anger

Does not hide its secrets.

It advertises itself
like a bad movie poster
luring the foolish into its stupid dramas.

Angry eyes, full of fire
propel heat outward
so everyone in our path
feels its rude accusations.

Our cutting voice and biting words
bludgeon those we target
leaving bruises that sting.

When we fall under anger's grip
we are oblivious to its power over us
clueless to the distorted, sickening lens
we hold to reality.

Anger's heat is so addictive
it lures many slaves to feed its fire;
they become addicts of injustice
serving tirelessly with burning hearts.

Anger addicts make dozens of little wars
to occupy their days
and find many willing converts
to their violent fever.

Even when silent
the weight of anger's fury
sends notice to all in our path
and leaves burdens of regret.

Regression

When things get intense and heated
or we feel wounded

We may misjudge the signs
let fears take over our mind
and revert to primitive reasoning.

Once we are hooked
and let our triggers take control
we fall back into old dramas
flail those we blame with harsh words,
work to undermine them
and gossip spitefully for added effect.

When the dust has settled
and we survey the damage
we may find many losses resulted
from our childish hissy fit.

Then spend months or years
trying to repair the damage,
hoping to get back to square one.

We may blame anyone or everyone possible
avoid those who witnessed our downfall

Or seek forgiveness
to not deepen our hole
and wait.

Uncentered

Few of us can stay true to our intentions
when faced with a person or situation
that opposes or doubts.

We frequently lose our footing
and backtrack
molding our actions to their pressures.

Even if our goal is altruistic —
showing compassion or making peace —
we may feel overcome by stress
and turn in another direction.

Most cannot stay true to our better wishes
in harsh conditions
we are too weak to see the path of light
when others fling shadows around.

So we lose our grounding
and work against our own purposes.

Chapter 3: Struggles

Therefore, if these long-lived, ancient enemies of mine,
The wellspring only of increasing woe,
can find their lodging safe within my heart,
What joy or peace in this world can be found?

Shantideva, The Way of the Bodhisattva
(8th Century)

Quiet

Is dangerous
that's why we hide from it
banish it to the bedroom
or lock it in the basement.

Quiet reveals troubles,
regrets, stupid mistakes,
damage.

Hidden meanings
come creeping out of the corners
to make us doubt our plans.

Quiet is really disturbing
with the people we love
because we need noise barriers
for emotional distance
but we seldom take them down,
living within walls of sound.

We become addicted to the safety
that constant drone seems to provide
needing the simplicity and comfort
of the usual messages
no need for messy questions,
we are right, after all.

Quiet requires trust
and so many of us have too little.

We see this scary world
full of threatening people
and block them out with devices

that murmur to maintain our comfort.

Some find the nerve
to push away the noise curtain
and hear the openings,
colors, textures, highs and lows
that are revealed by quiet.

Some of us fall in love with quiet —
sit with it
watch the sky change
get lost in it
and savor the rhythms of life.

But most find quiet disturbing;
too much unknown
too much unkindness
too much pain.

We run back behind the wall of noise
sink into the cloud of sound
and take noise weapons wherever we go
in case quiet lurks around the corner
to steal our happy lie.

Chaos

Is unavoidable pressure
like gravity
it pulls us down.

No matter how strong
our character and our path
chaos may grab us without warning
and take over.

The choices made by chaos
are not personal
it strikes rich and poor, old and young
upsetting our plans
stealing our treasures
rocking our foundations.

Some of us persist
find answers in the struggle
and get to a happier place.

Others don't have the strength to look
so remain childlike and injured
cursing the fates.

Dance Partner

Compelling eyes across the room —
Shall we take a risk?

Let's compare credentials
see if we should invest more time ...

Yes!

Be my dance partner
hold me tight and close!

Sway with me
to sweet melodies.

Mm-mm...

Stay in step
and balance my spinning.

Oh this romantic feeling
is too wonderful to ever stop!

Ah-hhhh...

Don't stand so close
give me a little room!

Let's do a little freestyle
and express ourselves.

Sigh...

You're supposed to
move like this!

Don't get in my way!
Jeez you are clumsy!

Phhhhtz!

Let's sit this next one out
I need to take a break!

Dancing just doesn't
seem interesting anymore.

Nahhhh...

You go!
I'll be alright...

I've got too much to do
to go dancing...

Ummm...

Remember when
we used to go dancing?

Tangles of Relationship

I. Sympathy

You look so despondent, dear friend.

How sad to see your weary face
and to hear that your relationship
has become a trap.

Long ago, your lover was
an angel promising rainbows
on the horizon of your life together —
bringing refuge from the sad lonely
and other specters of old age.

Now you have lost the glow of rainbows
and can only see dark clouds
limiting your sky,
the biggest cloud being your partner.

Your lover's luminescence
has become an ugly cartoon
all mouth and downward brow.

Their soul-warming words
have become icicles that jab
and leave you chilled.

You are despondent —
How did I not see this before?
Only my friends understand me.
My only peace is when alone!

So you hide, you numb,
you desperately seek escape.

II. Struggle

Now you are in the next phase
gray life with monster
with endless cycling misunderstandings
that mimic the sappage on TV.

You are not alone
millions face the same struggle —
my side versus your mean side —
inflaming each other's feelings
with pointed cuts and indignation.

This drama is so alluring, so addictive
you may never be free of it
unless you find its root inside.

Does your bag of tricks
hold anything besides a knife
and a one-way ticket?

III. Consider

This dark sky was painted by two hands
this relationship monster
was created by both of you
and both still feed it.

If you treat each other like enemies
the battle can only go on.

Projected fears gain much power
in reflecting off each other
then negative interpretations
push the toxic cycle on.

You both painted the heavenly vision
of your early relationship
before it got crushed
by pounding constant pettiness.

If you could free yourself now
you could dance into the future
with any partner.

IV. Distance

If you want another relationship movie
start with space
rest and cool your reactivity.

Stop filling the air with justifications and judgments
which make you blind and deaf
to your lover's good
as well as to openings for change.

Time and distance may help you to hear
what your partner has been trying
to tell you —
you've both ignored so many signs
on your road downhill.

V. Understand

Remove the anger mask
from your partner's face
reveal their softer feelings,
look into their eyes.

Anyone can act like a demon
when not heard,
when there is no consideration

for needs or pressures.

If you cannot tolerate your partner's flaws
if their human faults
bring you so much revulsion
the trouble lies inside you.

Your bitter obsessions
feed your misery more than they.

Try to bring in light
to illuminate their good side,
find some positive frames.

Human frailties are our work
there will always be more challenges —
we are infinitely complex
and constantly changing.

VI. Try Being Kind

Peace can only come
when we move beyond spite.

Try to be a friend to your partner
to be kind
no matter where you are going together
gentle friendliness can serve you both.

What is love
if it isn't kindness under duress
compassionate words during trouble?

That is how love heals
and it can heal this relationship too
even if you do not continue as partners.

VII. Peace

Relationships are the foundation
of peace in the world.

The world needs peace desperately
and relationship peace could show us
how to get there.

Please, make peace at home!
We cannot find peace out in the world
unless we make peace with each other.

Note: This poem was written for couples who are equals. When there is a marked social power difference, abuse or exploitation of either, its meaning does not apply.

Chain of Causality

We carry wounds from long ago
seeds of turmoil
that still itch and distract
and draw us to people
with the same itch configuration
and the same inner wars.

So we do battle over and over
with different people
who become the same adversary,
detractor, enemy,
whatever role keeps our drama going.

New souls keep taking our offered hand
for another fool's dance
so we smile and gaze at each other
until the knives come out.

Then the masks fall
and we realize
the foe we strike out at
is just like the one before.

Seeing that face again
we freeze, our defenses fail
and we become injured again
same place, same wound.

This chain of reactions could go on forever
hurt exchanged for hurt
blame exchanged for blame.

Who is the monster in our story?

A heroic clown?
A devilish magician?
A difficult parent?
Our wounded inner child?

There is no freedom
without unchaining ourselves
from every storyline of the past
that makes us blind to the present.

The healing process takes years
requiring constant work —

To see our dramas,
to understand our parts,
to forgive ourselves,
to value the good in our companions
and learn the power of kindness.

Relationship Insanity
(folie à deux)

As we spend years together
we rub off on each other
shaping one another's psyches
adding quirks and pressures.

We mix together idiosyncrasies
into a strange soup
flavored with the peculiar ways
of thinking, relating and living
that each of us brings
creating an odd reality of two.

Some relationship combinations —
worry and panic,
outrage and blame,
or disappointment and wallowing —
entrap us for years in descending spirals.

Couples who become confined
in those tiny co-realities
see only what fits the concepts and categories
of our reciprocal illusions.

Then judge and are judged
to fail those curious standards
bicker and bitch back
and crawl into retreat.

As we enter into these tunnels of love
we become enchanted
by the bizarre and petty rules
of our imaginary universes
distorting everything and everyone
outside.

Gender Mazes

Stereotypical male and female images
have entertained us for millennia
keeping most of us trapped
and ill at ease.

All through history
we soldiers of the binary gender role
have thought we were the only game
interpreting male and female markings
according to fixed rules
that have little to do
with the real hearts and spirits
of those who wear them.

Throughout those centuries
the other genders
were forced into the shadows
tormented, threatened, murdered,
whenever they tried to be seen
until fairly recently
when they started to break free.

These young rebels reject our straitjackets
refuse to wear them
and ask us to use different names.

Now we bear witness to the other genders
playing their parts in Earth's stories
of romance and adventure
dancing with partners
building families
playing old roles and building new ones
to find the love that they deserve.

We all are worthy of love
no matter the shape of our bodies
or the costumes we wear.

Women are men are women
or we are
something different,
something new,
something expanded,
something beautiful.

The Two Faces of Sex

Sex can be the bountiful giver
or the cruel user —
a dynamic river of energy
that brings vibrant new life
or a flood that overwhelms caring
leaving corpses swirling
in the pull of its currents.

I. Takeover

Procreation biology
molds every one of us to its purposes
then sexual fever draws us in
with nature's most powerful trickery

As the hormones of puberty
change us into sexual creatures —
re-shaping our bodies, minds, emotions
and desires.

We become frantic to join the mating game
obsessing about appearance rituals
facial markings, hair,
starving and pumping bodies,
making ourselves into plastic dolls

To then cover with cheap costumes
and parade for the meat market
so others can admire, leer,
and make degrading comments.

All to be assessed as sex-worthy
adequate for someone's sexual use
as we pray not to be a thing of pity or derision

among our target consumers.

II. Sexual Games

Game playing takes over interactions
as we perform popular scripts
for moving in for the score.

For many, love is the lure in sex's trap
as we pursue our lovers' hypnotic kisses
not seeing they hide teeth
that eat love for breakfast.

Only the most artful
can push away those luscious lips
when they start sucking.

III. Hurtful Games

For all history, we have enticed each other
with sex's elusive, simple thrills
and played tantalizing sex games
for the hidden purpose of submission.

Some become servants to lovers' whims
accepting control to avoid abandonment
becoming circus performers hoping to please
while repressing their shame
about being valued as objects
knowing their controllers have no concern for them.

A few practice domination
that is criminal in its cruelty
enslaving the bodies of the young and poor
to sell them as objects, for use and abuse
(while we turn our heads).

We hope their victims can find a way
to pull up from sex's quicksand
to reclaim their bodies, their minds,
and their goodness,
to get their wholeness back.

IV. Sex with Love

True lovers know the power of sex
and choose to remember
their partners are precious.

They enjoy sex's magnetism
but know it is secondary
to love's purposes.

Such lovers gaze into each other's eyes,
and sweetly connect
with the soft breath of spring
staying rooted in love's power
while remembering that sex is living energy
that nourishes and tests all lovers.

*This poem is dedicated to my clients who were, and are, rape
and incest survivors, prostitutes, abusers, and sex addicts. God
bless them for their courage! May their healing continue.*

Masculine Power

Is rooted in ancient survival struggles
that put fierce masks on men's faces
that we fear to look behind.

Social systems give masculine people
more rewards for their ambition and work
in every place on Earth
even when they are rude, unattractive or old.

Soldiers of masculinity seek power instinctively
and if others are foolish enough
to give it, or lose it
they'll take advantage with wicked pleasure.
leaving others in their dust.

Trapped in masculinity's narcissistic embrace
they push, push for more
taking up more and more space
that forces others to become small
as that reflexive male shoving forward
creates victims and enemies.

The most primitive masculine warriors
see everyone as enemies —
females, children, subordinates, animals,
are viewed as trivial, worthy of abuse
to be punished for softness and openness
as targets of angry outbursts.

The cost of this hyper-masculine thinking
is constant wars of control
in which no one is trusted
the horrors of violence are used
whenever convenient

and the suffering of collateral victims
is accepted as unavoidable.

Millions of both genders fall victim
to these gender-power games
enduring constant wounding
that never completely heals.

We are fascinated with this power dance,
spending great chunks of time
watching these wars on stages, screens,
public spaces and homes,
while refusing to look at causes
or speak of the scars that men carry
from unimaginable suffering.

This blindness keeps us colliding
counting our losses,
and divided against each other.

If we don't move past these ancient, futile ideals
and fearful, heroic myths
that celebrate masculine power and aggression
we will keep laying our world to waste.

Emotional Numbing

We often hide in clouds of dullness
whether closing our eyes to reality
or gliding over life's bumps
with drugs, fads and smokescreens.

Numbness is an easy escape
from life's many problems
and common horrors.

We don't want to be present
to feel whatever is done to harm
others around us
or ourselves.

So we sleep through life
riding these buffers
deadening our sensory connections
dulling our critical thinking
sacrificing love and joy.

Sickness

A heavy cloud descends
with pain, weakness, incapacity,
straining bodies and relationships.

Sickness can take many forms
bringing specific pains
general wretchedness
and possible body damage,

While our life force is taxed, depleted,
reducing our vitality and resistance,
taxing our self-care,
further weakening us.

We must ask for support to heal
but those who love us must choose
how much to caretake and sacrifice
and how much to listen to their limits
to protect their own health.

Sickness tests
our relationships
our lives
our faith
our well-being
and our purpose.

Aging

Brings many gifts
greater capacity, skill
broader knowledge
and blessed understanding
of the strange creatures
and landscapes around us.

But, aging also steals from us.

As we admire the latest prize
something else slips out the back
to be replaced with cheap replicas
that we don't notice
until we look closely.

The freedoms of youth slowly disappear —
clear glowing skin
strong pearly teeth
physical strength
wide open futures.

Or any moment, we may discover
lost attractiveness, lost accuracy,
lost respect.

Other losses are more violent
as friends, lovers, relatives,
whole groups
are taken from our lives.

Households of people gone
even our beloved communities morph
into something unrecognizable

Where is that comforting spot?

Then thoughts disappear
names, words, details,
dimming our minds.

Each loss a heartbreak
hundreds, thousands of them
some we fight
some we let go of
some we give up in despair.

But we cannot turn back
only step deeper into dry wilderness
where the landscape slowly empties
becoming desolate and grey
with fearsome creatures
lurking and howling around us.

The journey of aging wears us down
and though pain recedes sometimes
it will punch us in the gut again
so we must struggle to stay positive.

We can help each other hold on
if we manage to stay loving
through constant hassle draining
the decay of our bodies
and the heartache of dearest losses.

Thankfully
dazzling wisdom about life's mysteries
comes, at times
lighting up our past darkness
and creating new hope for our legacy.

That knowledge redeems us
frees us from the prisons of the past
and reminds us about the sweetness
of small things
beneath the shining, sheltering sky.

God Bless Us When We Fail

To say the kind thing
and fire out ugly words instead.

Help all of us who push away others —
to think before acting or speaking
to hear and honor those we love.

God, please help us
when we take advantage of someone
tell a lie or push our way
to find the healing of fairness.

Whenever we are careless
and leave hurt behind
bring us understanding and wisdom
to do better.

God, please send us comfort
when we lose our nerve
and don't share the words
that might heal a relationship.

Whenever there is an opening
in the walls with someone dear
help us speak.

God, please help us face the tests
of living our better intentions
and help us find courage
to see our actions with each other clearly
but with forgiving hearts.

Chapter 4: Failures

You know, it's quite a job starting to love somebody.
You have to have energy, generosity, blindness.
There is even a moment, in the very beginning,
when you have to jump across a precipice:
if you think about it you don't do it.

Jean-Paul Sartre, Nausea (1938)

Walls

There has been a wall growing between us
week by week
during the years of our relationship —
we both have contributed rocks.

A stony barricade
now towers between us
blocking our faces
and dimming our voices.

We won't take the wall down
because it might crush our hands
and we care too much
to add to each other's bruises.

Years ago we pounded these rocky barriers
with sledgehammers
but the debris made both of us bleed.

There is no remedy for these walls,
just a few gaps for looking through
to reveal soft eyes.

Parent-Child Burdens

The work of parenting is so demanding,
confusing and unceasing,
that it pushes many past their limits
bringing out fury and cruelty
or driving them to abandonment.

Parenting can wear anyone down
from its endless work
and so many knotty challenges
that eat away at the heart.

Then, a minor lapse of self-control
or a cry unheard or unheeded
can cause serious physical harm
deep emotional scars
or even death to the unlucky child
for a momentary slip.

These and a thousand trials gone wrong
become lifelong burdens of grief and guilt
that many parents carry
and the aching wounds of their children
who blame them for every scar.

Crushed

Disgrace falls on us without warning
an act of God, Kali and Coyote
all rolled into one humiliating episode.

Then we watch in horror
as our failings become stones
in the hands of those we love
for striking the monster they see in us
hoping to murder our dreams.

We may get pushed over the edge
by the weighty pressure of their hostility
and join them in the abyss of blame
where fear overwhelms faith
pain becomes burning
and good intentions become ashes

Or, we could choose to try kindness.

If the wisdom of experience
has given us the grounding to know
that blame brings nothing
but more loss and grief,
we may find silence is the best way
to let the angry storm pass
without adding to its thunder.

Though we are bewildered by their hate
there is no point in fighting
so we must stop ourselves from striking back
and surrender
tolerating the waves of shame
that keep coming

accepting that no one will listen.

This compassionate endurance
to bear another's hostile blaming
can be lonely and endless
though we may find comfort
with a few loyal friends
or the solace of prayer.

While we wait months, years,
for love's truth to be revealed.

Layers of Grief

Beneath these wars, murders and abuses
between nations, peoples,
family members, friends and lovers,
lay thousands of layers of unresolved grief
from 50,000 years of aggression and betrayal
against each other.

We each know them well
as perpetrators and victims.

We still practice treacheries daily
whether gossiping about a friend
manipulating the weak person at work
turning our backs on those who are down
or screaming at someone to
Do something about it!

The struggle to be loving
is forever burdened by grief's poisons
that keep us savoring the thrills
of aggression and fear
and holding onto wrongs
instead of moving on.

The layers of hurt may only keep growing
as we remain stubbornly arrogant
and refuse to put down our knives.

Old & Bitter

We can hold onto awful memories —
painful traumas, lost opportunities, betrayals...
and keep them alive inside
savoring them like vintage wine.

We may retell our sad stories
to work up maximum impact
to spread poison for wrongdoers
and wallow in sympathy for ourselves.

Success was denied by some evil bully
or twist of fate
and true love was snatched away
so we settled for this wretched life.

Meanwhile our bodies betray us with infirmities
and pleasures must often be denied —
dancing, travel, rich food…

Life's deficiencies
conspire to deny all good
and there is nothing left but misery

When love is not fought for every day.

Sad & Lonely

The mind plays tricks on us,
telling us what we expect to hear.

For the sad and lonely,
this becomes —
I never get what I deserve!
People are so hurtful!
Life is so unfair!

We chain ourselves to desolation
with self-centered wishing
and blame all those people
who disappoint.

Our negative thinking presses on others
pointing the finger at those who try to care
driving them away.

Sadness is a genius
at justifying self-pity.

The push and pull of that paranoia
drains and immobilizes us
trapping us in an unhappy room
where we long to leave
but fear moving.

Few find escape
from that lonely prison
because our narrow vision cannot see
outside.

Disappearing Women

In much of the world
women don't count —
we can be killed
as babies, girls, wives and widows,
or just disappeared
with little consequence.

Hundreds of millions of girls
are still pulled from school to work
condemned to be house slaves
or sold as sex slaves
so many shining eyes lost to history
with little chance of education
or mercy.

Centuries of slavery and oppression
have scarred every female
we feel that malice
even when it's not present
carrying it
within our biological, psychological maps.

Here in resource-rich countries
women are less often murdered or enslaved
but we find other ways to disappear.

Many fine women
feel we are not good enough
to be ourselves
to take up space
so we hide

Behind a male partner
who gives us a new name —

75

wife
Mrs. Him
caretaker of offspring
as worry and work take over our days.

Or, behind another dominator
who we shape our lives, values,
and time around.

Women lose track of ourselves
as others tell us how to be worthy
by serving their agendas pleasingly.

We fade and disappear physically too
hiding our features behind masks
plucking, shaving, torturing our hair
contorting our feet into sexy points
wearing flimsy, constantly changing uniforms

While many also shrink ourselves into thinner, bonier
more acceptable versions of female
we hope.

But for all this work
does anyone really see us?

What does the universe know of us
shrinking, hiding girls and women?

Many of us just slip away,
giving away
our names
our bodies
our voices
our laughter

our days.

Thus our world loses billions
of intelligent, funny, colorful voices —
spunky, opinionated girls
passionate young women
brilliant adults
wise older women —
and does not hear our urgent messages
and magnificent songs.

Racial Divisions

The privileges of light skin
have disconnected us
so profoundly
that vast numbers of us
remain unfeeling and ignorant
of the massive suffering
of the world's darker-skinned peoples
and how we contribute to it.

We keep them outside our comfort zones
preventing awareness and understanding
while every minute our boxes preach
more reasons to fear and despise them
with most *good* people listening
and nodding our heads.

Toxic social distortions fuel an immense scale
of scapegoating and violence
against our dark-skinned relations —
we crush their spirits
as we keep them chronically disempowered,
traumatized and erased.

Then we exploit our darker sisters and brothers
in thousands of ways
preventing access to good homes, good work,
good schools or fair services,
continuing a biased and punitive legal system
that puts millions in prison
to satisfy our hateful lies.

Thus many dark-skinned people feel desperate
and abandoned

because of our blindness to their pain
and our massive lack of compassion —
an enormous emptiness in our collective soul
that fuels cycles of suffering for billions.

Dr. King and others spoke of our long moral arc
but why have we done so little
to bend it forward in 50 years?

Why have we so often opposed fairness
for our darker-skinned relations?

Why don't we wish for their happiness?

Even after hearing their cries for 500 years
our racist fears and aversions
still gag and shackle our world
and every one of us.

Poverty

There are beautiful people all around us
sweet children, babies, idealistic young people,
and hardworking, good-hearted, gorgeous adults
of all ages,
who live in the constant misery of poverty.

Some of them don't please your sensibilities
but they've done nothing wrong
nothing we wouldn't do
if we were in their shoes,

Yet they are visited by hate every day
negative labels, rude bullying,
public harassment, screaming,
and a hundred other kinds of violence
against body and spirit.

They seldom know carefree times.

Even their innocents have their hopes crushed
in early years full of betrayals
by family, friends, public servants...
so many they hoped would offer rescue.

Our world creates many flavors of poverty —
sad neighborhoods, crumbling buildings,
schools of despair,
endless rip-offs, addictions,
and unrelenting sickness.

We spew the grime of our world
onto the faces of the poor
and lie to ourselves
that they don't feel it.

To Our Soldiers

You are in such a strange place
an insane, threatening world.

What good could we wish you
that would have any meaning?

Perhaps you would want to know
that we think of you
that we worry about your terrible risks
your loneliness
and about what war
will do to your heart.

That in wars created by the worst of us
you might forget the best in us —
the goodness in people
the thousand simple joys in life —
and turn into something hard
keeping awfulness forever inside.

Do what you have to, to survive
but even if you have to kill
don't become a killer

Don't give away your decency
whenever you have a choice.

Remember your friends and family love you
though they are far away
and cannot understand
the nightmare you are living.

Treasure your memories of home
they are real,

more real than this war
and the petty minds who designed it

And vastly more important,

Please don't forget your dreams
they are still the path to your healing
so fight for them.

Remember there is help
for traumatic memories and troubles
from those who do not hide from the truth.

Don't forget to tell your politicians
what you learned here
in their war
they need to know.

God keep you safe!

Cruelty

We notice cruelty
when it harms someone we care about
and may protest or try to stop it.

But cruelty is easy to tolerate
when its victims are outside
of our familiar circles.

Cruelty happens easily
when our victims don't matter
when we remain ignorant of their struggles
when we feel no responsibility to question
if we let ourselves be cruel.

Many of us stay cocooned
so others' suffering will seem unreal
screening their faces from our awareness
so we don't have to consider their torment.

On the small scale of this
we take advantage of others
for a moment's pleasure
belittle someone to improve our reputation
disrespect people for laughs
turn away when children or animals are abused
or ignore those who are down or lost.

Our careless encounters can crush
someone who is already low.

While large scale cruelties
are destroying our world
we don't care to see
how social choices and investments

play a part in that destruction —
gorging on the products of slavery
recklessly robbing land, air and water resources,
using predatory practices
to steal from the elderly and poor.

We feel entitled
to maintain our unsustainable ways
and refuse to see
the victims of our greed.

Over half the people of the world
are impoverished
imprisoned or enslaved
as we injure and traumatize nature
for our petty pleasures

Still we pretend
there are no consequences for our cruelty
turning our gazes away
and continuing to plunder.

Hate Rising

Social hatred has been growing
and it's everywhere we look
so ugly and frightening
that we're screaming and flailing
watching ourselves attack one another
with little thought to intervene.

The worst sicknesses of our way of life
are running wild —
addiction, narcissism, predatory greed,
senseless violence, hate propaganda,
and though these excesses
are tearing us apart
we want more, more, more …

We're adrift in confusion
can't find answers that work
that bring understanding
or ease our crazed striking out.

Love is the only power
that might slow our descent
into this madness.

But how can we remember love
while trapped in this horror movie
with so many terrifying monsters?

Perhaps we might look
beneath the demons' masks
to see the common human beings
behind each source of hate?

Without our fear and revulsion

they might lose their power.

If we really want to uproot hate
we must honestly reckon —
with the hate in our own hearts
with how we turn off our humanity to anyone
with how we believe any beings are unworthy
of God's blessings.

We must also face our indifference
to these evil practices
and recognize the useless suffering they cause
(theirs, and ours).

If we don't want to be one of the millions
of instruments of hate
in this era of shame

We can choose to reject hate
take our power back from hate
not practice or endorse hate
and not fall for enemy-making fear-mongers
so we can starve hate of our patronage.

Let us dedicate our energies to something better
to love, to God, to nature, to kindness
to a better world
and rediscover ways of respect and compassion
that guided us in gentler times.

Old Friend

I. Sweet Memories

Hello, old friend
your face is like a crystal ball
transporting my mind across the years
to a room filled with smiles and laughter.

People now long scattered are together again
eyes shining with enchantment
no thought to ever leave that sweet company.

We search the eyes of those innocents
sharing food, music, wisdom,
delighting in the flavors of many worlds
trusting utterly in our bonds.

What storm blew us apart?

II. Crash

Ancient troubles we all carry
in the marrow of our bones
made us blind and ignorant
of each other's lives,
so crashing was inevitable.

We felt immune to thousands of years
of misunderstandings and wars
between genders and cultures,
and became careless
allowing their ghosts
to creep into our fragile company.

Once awakened, these essence ancestors
dragged us into fear's vortex
where our caring pledges were no match

for its intensity.

So we turned our backs on each other
becoming victims and perpetrators
of another pointless war.

We are all humbled.

III. Solace

How sweet and sad
to see your face again, old friend.

We mourn the lack of means
to heal these tragedies
and share our lives again.

We are small pebbles on a long road.

We did no better or worse
than millions over history
who have faced such troubles
and forgotten how to be friends.

We hope some future generation,
will hear these shabby stories
and discover the path beyond our blunders

So our limboed grief
may find release.

Letter to Our Children's Children's Children

You must wonder about the people of our time —
What were they thinking?

How we could let things get so out of hand?
So brutal, so destructive, so greedy …

But we weren't thinking
about how many animals died for our petty comforts
or the lands wasted to boost our portfolios.

We allowed ourselves to be happy residents
of a culture that plundered
and spared nothing in our push to provide
for our excesses.

We failed to see the folly
of 4,000 civilizations before us
ruin after ruin
each one a monument to pride
silently witnessing our path to destruction.

We gained too much power
and became like animals
gripped onto our vast territory
consuming, destroying, desecrating
billions of Earth's treasures
while pride told us to not back up an inch.

We could not wait or listen
could not slow our abuse
ran straight into the abyss screaming
fist-raised and angry-faced
Don't take what is MINE!

Those of us who could see
were cowed by their threats
afraid of their rage.

A million acts of courage occurred
and we let them be ignored or crushed
to keep from becoming targets.

Our mistakes are in the records
(along with tricks that fed our ignorance)
our stupidity has not been silent.

Look at those errors without mercy
but don't think yourselves better.
We thought we were superior
to the savage barbarians of the past
but then became gluttonous and merciless —
the worst of history.

Many of us made sacrifices, small and great
to leave more for your time
dear grandchildren of our children
for what little that is worth.

And we mourned for you
grieving for the miseries and losses
that would come from the carelessness
we have practiced with your world
in our primitive age.

We thought of you with great sadness
and sent you loving prayers
for your survival and healing.

May our legacy,
the ragged earth you inherit
and the ghosts of our countless victims
help you remember to be thankful and humble
to honor those who resist the madness
and dare to join them.

Chapter 5: Lightening Up

You have to love. You have to feel. It is the reason you are here on earth. You are here to risk your heart. You are here to be swallowed up. And when it happens that you are broken, or betrayed, or left, or hurt, or death brushes near, let yourself sit by an apple tree and listen to the apples falling all around you in heaps, wasting their sweetness. Tell yourself you tasted as many as you could.

Louise Erdrich, The Painted Drum, (2005)

Lightening Up

Sometimes when we are down
we just need to change perspective.

When we are stuck in victim-thinking
or shamed about a stupid mistake,

We have to crack ourselves open
to other possibilities
and let go of the mindset
that says our errors must keep us down.

Laugh at the absurdity
of our self-important storyline
and the control we imagine having
since chaos always comes along
to tear apart our plans.

Instead,
let's enjoy life's simple pleasures —
the lift that comes with each smile we see
the music of laughter
the perfection of small details —

And allow something else to happen.

Laughter

Is a realization in our being
an awakening
to how temporary and trivial
our fusses are.

Laughter physically releases
emotional weights
dissipating their energy.

That's why we vibrate from within —
laughing frees our core
brings cleansing energy
and breaks up limiting resentments,
judgments and petty moods,
allowing relationships to reconsider
their sweet roots.

If we just let laughter come
we can share this bumpy journey
with our fellow passengers
and enjoy the exhilaration
of not knowing what dip or turn
may come next

In the crazy carnival ride
of relationship.

The Offensive Idiot Test

Everyone encounters selfish jerks
they are common as flies
and often found among coworkers, bosses,
neighbors, friends, family, and lovers.

How should we cope
when our turn comes?
When we're being belittled, ignored, or undermined
by the abusive fool of the day?

If we forget our value
we may apologize, whine,
and weaken our position.

If we forget our purpose
and get sucked into their sick logic,
we may turn into fellow harassers.

We can be light with it
make a joke back
to show we are equal
and unwilling to back down.

Pushy, rude people are one of the hardest tests
of who we are
and what we make of our lives.

It's all about one-upmanship
so don't play,
don't fight,
and don't submit.

Just laugh at the absurdity
of this bizarre power sport.

Remember, in the end,
the real test is whether
we sink to their level of behavior.

If we can remember
to stay respectful and kind
we have won
the more important battle.

Eluding Drama's Capture

Dramas don't care about anyone or anything,
their power drives a mighty riptide
that pulls many of us down.

When nerves are edgy,
when we don't feel right,
when we sense we are being pushed,
when we make ourselves sick with not wanting,

Drama sees an opening.

It triggers a hundred fantasies
of what might go wrong,
of bad motives, undeserved cruelty,
and blocked hopes.

Our world is full of such imaginary stories,
repeated cycles of unfairness,
using bits of reality as props.

We could ride the energy waves,
and hang on,
if we can calm down
and work to disarm our triggers.

Without fascination and horror
to fuel our emotional hooks,
these struggle cyclones will pass
from view,

So we can rise above
drama's wind, lightning and thunder
and become free
to make mindful choices..

Accident

So much of our lives result
from random twists of fate,
not intention or work.

Many of our lovers and friends
were balls tossed in the same scrambler
that somehow came out stuck together.

While many of our roles,
however fitting or disastrous,
have been those we fell into.

Even home can result from stumbling into a place,
whether gem or trap,
and staying.

Then life may, or may not, throw a bomb into our lives,
something or someone that upends everything
leaving us ragged,
but if it does, don't take it personally,
just compromise some balance
out of the rubble.

The winds of chance may shape us
more often than will or character,
making us revise our plans,
live with different possibilities,
and become different people.

Our judgment is often so faulty,
that can be a blessing...

Prayer to Shut Up

Dear God,
We pray to you to help us learn
to hold our tongues.

Please save us, Great Spirit,
from opening our mouths,
and saying something stupid,
again.

Give us faith, Great Mother
to keep our worries
to ourselves
and stay our need to fix things.

Give us patience, O Lord,
help us realize
we don't know what is right
for anyone else.

Help us, Dear Friend,
to let go of control
and relax.

It would be a blessing
to so many people.

Amen.

Chapter 6: Healing

Love makes your soul crawl out
from its hiding place.

Zora Neale Hurston,
Their Eyes Were Watching God, (1937)

Solitude

Do we have a need, a right, to be alone?
When a beloved wants our company,
can we say *no*?

How scattered we can become
in the chaotic push and pull of together time —
the demands, the chattering, the fussing ...

Open quiet is essential
to see things clearly
without other's pressure and distortions.

We need time alone to reflect
on the themes behind our problems
to examine our actions
and consider alternatives.

We need space
to pull together the pieces
to make sense of our messes

And to listen to the quiet workings
of heart and mind
that we may see our way to balance
and its serenity.

Space

I. Physical Space

Humans have constructed lines and boxes
to shape our movements
around and between
Earth's masses and waterways.

Earthy and man-made forms
constrain the patterns of living
physically determining how we flow and connect
to everyone and everything that matters.

These shapes and openings mold our consciousness
and set the stage for how we see reality
and what we block out
as not normal.

When physical space allows freedom of movement
visual space is clean and open
and auditory space is quiet
that helps us to work ourselves open
and to reconsider our directions
in this cluttered, colliding world.

II. Interpersonal Space

Distance and direction speak to our companions
about the state of our connecting
showing when we are open or closed
approaching or pushing away from another.

Spatial arrangement can reveal our frustration
or pleasure or sadness,
especially when accompanied by signals

of eyes, hands and face.

Relationship spaces demonstrate
our influence over others
convey our needs
(or invite others to disregard our needs)
and show concern or disregard for others.

The patterns and qualities of interpersonal spaces
hold many clues and wield great power,
so allowing ourselves to see and know space
will help us be a little less clueless
about the mysteries of relationship.

Anchors

Solid friends
supportive family members
leaders with integrity
and trustworthy healers or guides
can be anchors for us —

Psychological still points
to help us find grounding in this stormy life.

During waves of trouble
when disease or trauma diminishes us
or our vision becomes fogged,
anchors can guide us
or help us find our way.

They can provide calm refuge
for resting and thinking
restoring our sanity
remembering our purpose
recovering our sense of goodness
and finding the best way to go forward.

If good people are not available
books, writings, music,
places of spirit, gardens, wilderness and trees,
almost anything that inspires
can provide that grounding
while animals can be anchors
of love and protection.

We can be anchors for others also
whenever we are able
to help those we care about
find their way home.

Friends

When family judges our curious gifts
when romance crashes or disappears
when work or illness bring us low
friends can be our solace.

Friends can often hear what matters
when lovers and family are deaf.

The support of friends
grounds and nurtures us
during many hard times.

Friendship can expand other relationships
and build respect between family members,
coworkers, neighbors, lovers or ex-lovers,
transforming them into something more equal
and accepting.

We can hold onto friendships
despite inconvenient differences
and bewildering needs,
if we can compromise
and wait respectfully.

When friends join energies
with compassion and kindness
our troubles become lighter
the radiance of love grows
and we are healed.

Apology

We fail each other every day
between error and disregard
but too many of these failures
can break a relationship apart.

Some lapses cut deeply
others push too far
and our hearts are often too reactive
and untrusting
so a wall grows with every mistake.

Apology may stop the hands from adding a brick
or take one away
before cementing them in.

Those who care for us need a gesture
of understanding
acknowledging our slip of consideration
their feelings, their anguish,
and our desire to not repeat.

Apology shows compassion for their experience,
with some careful words
and humility.

We cannot control what others hear
just sincerely try to touch their pain
and show that their happiness
is treasured.

Forgiveness

Is a struggle against fear
that wants to bury all wrongs
in a nameless grave.

When we see we have given
so much power to the past
we can make a choice
to stop counting wrongs
and gift ourselves with a lighter spirit.

Forgiveness takes a leap into the unknown
choosing to rise above the gloom
in trust there is a better way.

Some of us are too locked up inside
to consider forgiveness work
so first must do the work of healing.

Others are challenged with how to pardon
remorseless people who abuse their power —
might forgiving condone their behavior
and allow them to do more wrong?

We can release our grief
without minimizing offenses,
and find understanding for the damage
that made them this way,
while still knowing that justice
is the only way to freedom
from whatever is driving them to these wrongs.

Most difficult is forgiving ourselves,
because fear and shame are excruciating

to face.

These and all of our tired burdens —
the terrible times, the struggles,
the holding back —
can be released
and the dams inside can break down,
to let tears rain like waterfalls
into the hollows within.

Love requires us to go beyond our limits
to rise above the hurts we encounter
in our broken world,
and find forgiveness
again, and again, and again.

To Those Left Behind

We ask your forgiveness
for any discomfort we caused
by leaving your company
so abruptly.

If our leaving was roughly done
we are deeply sorry.

Withdrawing was the best choice then
for maintaining inner balance
and we regret it caused you pain.

Relationships constantly constrain us
with demands, moods and thought-frames,
but we also are driven to be free
when expectations are too heavy,

So we may do something wild
to shock ourselves away
or drift quietly into separation.

You are good people
kind in many ways
we truly regret your disappointment
and our failings.

We hope somehow, someday,
to find the way back to friendliness
and mutual healing —
to leave a good mark on our connection.

Misunderstanding - Understanding

When we are unable to find mercy for another
we push them away
closing our hearts another bit
and making ourselves more brittle
and isolated.

To turn around misunderstanding
takes daring, determination
and compassionate digging,

To hear each other's meanings
and bear each other's darkness.

Understanding requires effort
to not block others out
constantly rebuilding doors and windows
between us
being patient till both are able to see
something that might keep us linked.

When we find that clear window
into another's heart and mind
it brings healing relief to both
and deepens our bonds with all humanity.

Discernment

Is often confused with judgment
because they are similar processes
save the boxes that come with judging.

Both involve observing and analyzing
but judgment fixates on the flaws
to see who is unworthy of concern,
while discernment keeps looking
because flaws do not get one
pushed away.

Discernment looks at the whole —
the subtle workings of shadows and light
the colorings of feelings
the intensity of stress
the burdens, the illusions
the blocked channels and choked voices
and the intentions behind it all.

Discernment does not close the door and hide
it knows we are all sinners.

It looks for needs and possibilities
to assess what might make harmony
or what might bring grief.

Discernment gently pushes away when needed
to protect boundaries,
sharing the reasons
so striving can continue
in the light of concern.

Harsh Transition

I. Impact

There is raw pain at the moment
when unexpected cruelty
rips open our fleshy coverings.

Burning nerve ends flood us
second by second
waves of unendurable pain
block every good thought.

Can we stand it?
That is the only need
to bear grinding pain
to find the courage to not regress
and destroy our moorings in panic.

The easy distractions have costs —
drugs, blame, even escape fantasies
separate us from knowledge
and push away those who care.

We must search for something good to hold onto —
a faith, a friend, a book,
a garden, a spiritual belief,
a view of the future.

Dig inside for meaning
figure out what matters
focus on that.

If there's no time for that now
and no clarity,
we must simply wait

for the burning to pass
and give way to cool breezes again.

II. Recovering

When there are openings for thinking again
we may reconsider our ruined walls.

Even if it was a horrible nightmare
and we were lucky to survive,
our reactions to the trauma process
hold clues to our character;
evidence of strengths and blindnesses
so when we can,

Look.

The evidence is easily lost
if we turn away.

We can become archaeologists,
combing fingers through debris
for the shards that explain our mysteries.

It helps to be soothing
as we do this disturbing review —
to encourage ourselves through pain
to find clarity
for discerning what we need to do.

If we respond gently
to our own errors,
being as soft and caring
as we would to any fallen child,
we might never doubt we are worthy.

III. Remember

Tragedy teaches us to be grateful
for everyone and everything
that matters in this life
while preparing us for the sorrows
of later years.

It presses us to find sweetness
in the small moments between.

No matter how blessed
or well-constructed our life may be
a turning will come
when we will be grateful
to have known the taste of loss,

And will treasure our tender scars
for the stories they have to tell
of our strength
in the face of devastation.

In the Middle of Catastrophe

I. Trusting Love

Misfortune eventually crashes down
on all of us without warning,
and stays
often suppressing our efforts
to rise from our miserable ruins.

It is then we need love most —
in the middle of bodies failing
in horror and humiliation
or when much that we treasure
is coming apart before our eyes.

We must hold onto love then
as the brutality of tragedy
is pounding us low
and push aside our egos
to ask for love's gentle healing.

Love can help free us
can loosen our guarding
so we can fall apart in safety
grieve
rest
and reconsider our best good.

If our intimates are also caught
in trauma's downward suck
only offering crumbs
we must look elsewhere
to find the support we need.

II. Giving Love

We must also give love
to others suffering trauma's blows
supporting our connections
as they support and nurture us.

It is not easy

To screw up our courage
deny our cowardly escape wishes
and go to those we love
in their most wretched hour
to hold their hand and say
I am here.

Whether we are heroic or terror-filled then,
whether we can muster good words or not,
these moments
last for centuries.

Love Will Save Us

I. Test of Aging

If time beats us down
and we cannot shake our resentments
feeling every mishap as personal
until bitterness takes over our minds
suppressing every mercy and smile

We may harvest failures,
lost friends and lovers,
disappointments magnified
dreams forsaken.

Seeing our lifetime of mistakes and losses
without compassion
can push the best of us over the edge
into the quicksand of regret.

But it's never too late
to turn from misery to love —
it can ease our final years
when facing increasing losses
and the terror of falling apart.

Love provides a way to soften our declining
so even we, life's greatest fools
can find refuge
if we give voice to our caring
and release our resentments.

As we age, we are challenged
to create love
to nurture love's promises

and share them generously

To give our time
to be big-hearted
even when we are disregarded
and to show brilliant gratitude
for the gifts we receive and witness.

II. Test of Dying

The process of our dying
however arduous or brief
can be a gift or a curse.

Our dying hour leaves a legacy to our companions —
a pointed middle finger
a guilt-inducing moan
or a loving, wishful smile.

Will we scream bloody murder
when our turn comes?

Or let ourselves go into life's steamy brew
with loving intentions and faith?

Let us remember to live love to the end —
to be generous, kind and thankful
whenever possible
and work to support the circle of compassion

So we can leave the world a little softer
by the way we let life go.

A Little Wisdom

The wreckage of our lives —
our legacy of failures, duds and half-successes —
is the price we've paid
for a little of wisdom's gold.

Every bit of wisdom we gain
costs us dearly in sweat and humiliating folly
that seems endless
but each revelation can have
enormous soul-saving value

As it helps us
avoid another stupid, selfish act
turn away from emotional sabotage
or to hold back an idiotic opinion.

Each lesson we learn is precious
as it keeps us from losing friends
or breaking hearts
and yields bounties of sweetness.

Prayer for Balance

Dear Guiding Spirit, please help us
to remember to honor our limitations.

Help us to see the difference
between generosity of heart
and not letting others do their work.

Help us to see and overpower insecurities
about our place in relationships
that compel us to give in
or grab too much.

Help us stop looking for what we can get
and give with gentle respect.

Help us find a balanced way to be with others
so that we are nourished
and they are honored
through healthy connections.

Help us to see the humanity
of those who walk with us
instead of guarding against them.

Help us to remember
that we are all lost together
in this ridiculous predicament
and cannot find our way out
without love in balance —
the only thing that lasts.

Chapter 7: Opening

*To love means to open ourselves to the negative
as well as the positive — to grief, sorrow, and
disappointment as well as to joy, fulfillment,
and an intensity of consciousness
we did not know was possible before.*

Rollo May, Love and Will (1969)

Changing

Our brains arrange our thinking
around early coping,
using old strategies over and over
throughout our lives.

These primitive patterns hold on
trapping our spirit
and constraining our relationships,
but we often cling to them
regardless of the suffering they cause
for decades,
because we can't imagine different ways.

Old habit patterns often lead to messes
that repeat, again and again, during our lives
and they may keep us
from ever reaching our dreams.

We can look down the road honestly
and imagine how our story
will play out those patterns,
then wonder —
Is that what I want?

We can choose
to defy useless habits,
and experiment with different ways,
practicing the best ones
until they settle in gently.

The people around us
may not be pleased by our changes
but they'll come along eventually
(or not)

as we evolve our relationships.

By giving ourselves the power of change
we can overcome the unhappy past
and build sweeter stories.

Vulnerability

Love demands we open
to those we love
reveal what is behind our masks,
though every opening is a risk
of falling into darkness.

Vulnerability is easy for the young
before inevitably, human carelessness
proves what thoughtless jerks we are.

Later in life, many of us
shut our doors and windows
to the harsh weather
that comes from our beloveds'
careless messes.

It takes great determination and courage
to release our pretences
and reveal our nakedness
to our beloveds.

Continually opening to discomfort
is the common lot of lovers.

Finding Answers

Analyzing, judging, grasping,
gnawing away at life.

We struggle constantly
hoping to find something —
our purpose, some meaning,
anything,
that could settle our restless minds.

We chase the elusive forever lover
slave for a beautiful garden and home
travel to yearned-for destinies
struggle to understand problems
strive for mastery of skills.

Even when accomplished
none of these fulfill us for long —
the happiness is temporary,
and our troubled mind wants more.

The contentment we do find
sometimes can be so fragile it shatters.

There we are, at some desired destination,
and the shininess drops away
revealing shallowness all around
empty smiles, empty words...
What am I doing with these zombies?

Leaving does not resolve anything —
the hunger follows us to the next place
and finds another reason to ache.

The question is not

What's wrong with these people
(or places or things)?
but,
Where does my unhappiness really come from?

Finding clues to this question
can take years, decades.

We can only wait
for our hearts to release their secrets.

Being Single

Is the ultimate gift
of space.

No matter the reasons behind it
(failures, rejections, choices...)
being single frees us
from the scrambled energies
of being in relationship.

Singleness provides space
for healing the restrictive knots of early years
giving us time to nurture ourselves
into greater wholeness.

Being single gives us generous openings
for softening hard edges
for unfolding oneself more fully
for friendly unraveling
of the threads of imagination, mind, and spirit,
so we can discover new ways.

Single years
may yield the deepest fulfillment
and bring us wisdom,
lightness and bliss
(or not).

Yet, many are unwilling
to savor their time as singles
and hurry back
into the work of relationship.

Truth

We must not think we know the truth
or that it is easy to see.

There are 10,000 frameworks of understanding,
10,000 veils that come and go,
that apply and don't apply
and millions of known and unknown factors
between ourselves and the universal reality
the mystery that we live within.

We pick out what is comfortable —
the familiar, what we've known —
needing to validate our beliefs
and not challenge ourselves.

That past-comfort-pressing
keeps us lost to the moment
blind to what's really out there —
the grit, the hurt, the unexpected.

We may only hear truth
when our personality is shocked
when reality kicks our comfort in the pants
and bewilders our minds with the unfamiliar.
That's good!

Being jolted by truth
helps us break up old thinking
and become astonished
by how much more we can see
(a little more awake, a little less dead).

Seeing the uncomfortable truth
can push our minds

beyond the confines of our patterns
forcing our ego prison a little wider.

Truth is bigger than all of us
as far-reaching as the universe
and likewise expanding.

Consciousness

Is mind-vision —
seeing and feeling life as it envelopes us,
without losing ourselves in it,
or in the 50,000 distractions
that constantly pull us away
from real knowledge and real contact.

We have been asleep —
constantly letting others tell us
what to think.

I. Truth

Consciousness is a dedication to truth
as it manifests.

To be fully conscious —
we must challenge the veils of our minds
and the boxes of mass thinking
to see behind and beyond them
not falling onto the easy lies
that keep repeating
(money, sex, gender, aggression...),
developing awareness of our blinders.

This gives us the power
to move freely around the world
and to open doors that have been closed.

Holding our minds open
is immense and difficult work

as our mental muscles are not accustomed
to restraining our mindframes
in order to question and choose.

II. Social Awareness

Thousands of pressures shape our thinking
tethering us with should messages
and urgings from everyone in our landscape
to be who they think we should be
(an ordinary fool).

And we do the same to everyone we interact with
pushing them into comfort categories
and judging them when they don't fit
or won't go.

If we could renounce these objectifying habits
we might see the people before us
without turning them into enemies
or things to use —
see others as whole, worthy of respect,
no matter their disconnect and neglect.

Freeing ourselves from these many pulls
lets us join with people
become allies and friends
and receive mountains of riches
from truer connections.

III. Fire of Consciousness

Consciousness shapes us with fire —
internally, interpersonally, globally,
changing everyone and everything it touches.

To practice conscious witnessing
don't struggle with what is seen
just let impurities be there
let everything be there —
the good, the ugly, the messy,
the compassionate, the mean-spirited,
the terrified, and the many, many blessings.

Witness everything without prejudice
without preference
and find its balance within natural cycles.

We can also use group consciousness
to support the good in our universe —
that which is kind, nurturing, generative —
by identifying that goodness
linking minds, eyes, hands,
and sending our love fire to it.

In 10,000 Years

Will some space alien archaeologists
or mutant humanoid researchers
dig through our rubble and find
a digital treasure trove
from the 21st century?

Will they sift through trillions of zettabytes
of bizarre and fantastic videos,
emails, blogs, vacation scenes,
social networks, news-spin,
celebrity scandal and music?

Will their archaeological institutions
display our internet pages and profiles
with translations and cultural references?

Will they see collections
of Ancient Earthling Literature —
distilled wisdom and advice,
thriller, zombie and chick-lit genres,
survivor stories and character-trashings?

Might they discover some of our heroes
and antiheroes?

Will they be mystified by our vast capacity
for unmitigated self-destruction?
Or, will they see a striving complex world
whose blood was sucked dry?

Will they teach their children stories
of our self-destructive excesses
to caution them?

Will they avoid our fate?

Prayer for the Invisible

Please God,
protect those who are lost and forgotten.

When anyone is neglected or abused
send them comfort
and remember them
when we do not.

God, please take care
of all the wounded, struggling people
we don't want to see —

The sad old people longing to be touched
the millions terrorized by violence
the refugees hiding from our scorn

The countless lost souls in prisons
warehoused away from our thoughts

The homeless in the rain and cold
the desperate parents who cannot pay their bills
the bullied workers, the starving villages

The millions of unprotected children
the angry lost teens

The sex slaves
the mind-numbers
the untouchables
the many people bashed around in the shadows

And so many who cannot speak their suffering
behind walls of numbness.

Sometimes our own loved ones
become lost behind unfeeling walls

kept at a distance from our hearts.

All these invisible ones are part of us
(and part of you, God)
their suffering pulls and pushes on each of us
their beings are woven into the fabric of our universe.

Great souls hear their voices and cry for them,
why can't we?

God, please help us not turn away
from the sad souls at the edge of our world,
help us reach through our walls of ignorance
to let the invisible know they are not alone.

Please help us
to see them
to listen to their voices
to learn about their plights
and to keep them alive in our concerns.

Help us to do what we can
to stop the hurting.

God, please help us
honor the invisible as your children
to remember they deserve happiness
as people with hopes and fears
just like us.

That would be such a gift
to them and to us,
making our hearts pulse with life
and empowering us
to begin healing the whole world.

Chapter 8: Being

Love without role, without power plays,
is revolution.

Rita Mae Brown,
A *Plain Brown Rapper* (1976)

The Road Continues

Once we decide to share relationship's road
then we must decide how to be —
how to travel with this person
while sharing this long journey?

How should we proceed
when the weather between us shifts
from sweetness to iciness
to heat?

And how do we cope with the many costs
and troubles we encounter
during our travels together?

The road to love is rarely without breakdowns
so we have to stop sometimes
to listen and consider our errors
with full attention.

We may not want to endure
the rough parts of relationship adventures,
preferring easy driving on smooth highways.

But if we are seeking more than empty horizons
if we want to discover exotic places
and befriend interesting people on the way
we must keep going

Pushing through relationship muck
and rising above mountains of troubles
to savor the sunny stretches and gorgeous views
of a shared journey.

Family Love Patterns

Whether our family was —
a safe haven of caring
a pleasant conforming box
an idiot's nest of drama
or an icy cave —
it was our school for love.

All of our patterns of seeking closeness,
communication skills, trust issues,
tolerance capacity,
biases and reflexive reactions,
were molded by family interactions and pressures
evolving over generations.

So that a mean family teaches meanness
often so well
that we will struggle against meanness every day
even decades later.

And so it goes
with depressed or cold or anxious family patterns
each marking a lifetime of relationships
and self-care.

Once we become comfortable in these dramas
we turn new intimates into parents and siblings
continuing the same roles
with whatever emotion cycling we've known
(criticizing, shaming, pleasing, using…)

But if we want a sweeter life
we can write new storylines
learn gentler ways to live together
and create nurturing partnerships

with old and new families
of blood and heart.

Compassion

Notices others' troubles and pain
and feels touched by their predicament.

Compassion moves us to show caring
for every defeated soul
whose suffering we witness
affirming they are worthy
of loving responses.

Compassion wants to reach out
to help people, relationships, and the world
to heal from the stains of wrongdoing
to encourage our weary spirits to heal
and have faith.

Compassion gently connects us all
with fundamental acceptance, caring
and feelings of peace.

Love is a commitment to compassion
a commitment to care
to seek understanding of our beloveds
no matter how they might
push our buttons
or pull apart our safety nets.

Kindness

Is love in motion
giving sweet comfort
to the weary souls it touches,

Reaching beyond the selfish ego
to consider others' needs
not wanting anyone to suffer unnecessarily
and helping without asking for payback.

Where there is conflict
kindness empowers understanding
restores goodwill
and plants the seeds of forgiveness
dissolving our divisions.

Kindness is not easy —
the self-fulfilling thing
we want to do instinctively
may not be kind,
so we have to reconsider our actions
and find what is best for all.

Kindness is open, compassionate
generosity of spirit
that lights the path between people and cultures
showing us the way to peace.

Gratitude

Is an awakening
that rouses us from our common daydreams
to acknowledge the value
of all that touches and supports us.

Gratitude recognizes life's many gifts
that bring beauty into our lives
then sends sweetness back.

Being thankful has immense power
to redeem us from bitterness and despair
and to bring in peace and lightness
(if we let them in).

Gratitude is the root of love
grounding us in the perfection all around us,
providing support and welcoming.

Gratitude is the work of love
a refusal to take anyone or anything for granted
or use them without thought.

Gratitude is also the fruit of love
nourishing the hearts of those we honor
feeding them sweetness and delight.

It is only with unrelenting appreciation
that love can stay happily alive.

Presence

Is so frequently ignored
in matters of love

Because without it
we forget to be there
in the room
and let our minds travel
through vast regions of space
avoiding contact
Uh huh…

Or we forget to stay home
driven to outside scenes
neglecting our base.

To be present means staying in contact
through stressful times, foul moods,
pain, and whimsy,
in order to share our truths
our most mundane thoughts
and other daily energy emanations
to link spirit to spirit.

Presence is a commitment
to sharing the grit of life
and finding its meaning together.

Being present now
allows us to experience the many gifts
that come with each person, place or thing
that touches us.

Chapter 9: Magic

Love works magic.
It is the final purpose
Of the world story,
The Amen of the universe.

Novalis /
Georg Philipp Friedrich Freiherr von Hardenberg,
Blüthenstaub-Fragmente (1798)

Peace

Is always waiting
behind the noise

And raises its sweet arms to embrace us
whenever we tire of fighting
and look across the room.

Peace is determined
to overcome our limits of acceptance
believing none should be beaten down
and all guided to share our good.

The vision of peace
sees everyone and everything
as worthy, even sacred —
every whiny child, old fool, ugly creature,
hideous alcoholic, arrogant bully and ripoff artist.

Peace understands
that every horror that we suffer
comes from ancient survival habits
and focuses on disconnecting the link
between power and violence.

Peace asks us
to find tolerance for the foolishness of youth
the difficult words of dissidents
and the messes of life.

The wisdom of peace urges us
to open our hearts and minds
to listen to one another's feelings
and to make space for each other.

Peace gently moves us towards healing
helping love flow more freely
less encumbered by fear.

Beauty

Has the power to awe,
move us, and draw us in.

Beauty of appearance
(natural or contrived)
brings pleasure and a sense of goodness
while enchanting our eyes and minds.

But we may become greedy and grasp for beauty
try to define or control it
making all involved sick
as beauty is extracted, mass-produced,
distorted and misused.

We forget our eyes have the power
to see beauty in anything —
a bug, a parking lot, a dead flower —
by adjusting to see the perfection.

The power of beauty really comes
from the perceiver —
from attitude
from openness to the moment
from curious acceptance
that everything has its own fulfillment.

Inner beauty grows from using this vision
to see the beauty in everyone and everything
and sharing that view.

Beauty is ultimately finding what is missing
then arranging things together
so spirit can be revealed
and find its own expression.

Precious

When time or wisdom
finally helps us to drop our foolish burdens
of resentments and petty wishes

We may finally see the beautiful souls
of all our dear companions —
working courageously
and generously loving
despite this bumpy, sweaty life.

Tearful joy may overwhelm us
when we awaken
to our cherishing of our companions.

For a moment, this clarity
may stop our begrudging
of each other's common weaknesses.

We pray we can manage
to stop creating obstacles
and make a commitment
to add something.

This Moment

This straining, messy,
awful moment in time

Is perfect.

If we could push aside our agendas
for a second,
we'd find perfection
bursting out of its confines.

There are numerous signs, here and now,
that teach so profoundly
that validate the strengths we hold inside
that let us know who we really love
and what we need to say.

This moment brings truth
illuminates weaknesses
and builds knowledge and wisdom
making us stronger.

If we can make ourselves look
at the clues
at the whole picture
how everything fits together
we might discover where our path is leading
and how to join love's direction

So this moment can rise up
riding a cloud of joy
and heal.

We

Can shut people out
with walls and gates
but we are still connected
to every starving baby
and suffering being on Earth
by the energy dynamics of our lifestyles
our grand history
and our future fate.

We can use sophisticated machines
to purify our air, water and food
but we are still connected
to every poisoned land and fouled water
by our reckless practices.

They will feed us back
what we feed them.

Our habits shape our world —
from the earth under our feet,
to the atmosphere that we breathe
and the people around us.

The future will not let us escape
what we do to each other,
to the planet and her life forms.

When any form of life suffers,
the fabric of our universe
is wrenched like a wet rag —
the more suffering anywhere
the more twisted we become.

When life is supported
in the smallest ways
the life-stream fills,
brightens, pulses,
and softens.

So we must look at every action
think how it affects the forces of life
see how it connects to everything
and ask

What could be hurt by this?

The future will speak of our abuses
as well as our gifts,
what will it say of you and me?

Not one of us is separate or alone
the world hangs on our ankles
we are always pulling and pushing at each other.

These energies entwine us
with complex emotional channels,
thought-streams,
and chemical, vital exchanges
making us inseparable.

But when our minds come together
immense power generates
things move, old forms break apart
and we evolve.

Background Notes

While I have written a number of articles over the years, I was reluctant to become a poet and it happened somewhat by accident. My love of words has always driven me to try to sort things out on paper and finally that exploded into poems. I had written only a handful of poems before 2007, but then started writing dozens about the amazing things I've been witnessing, primarily from experiencing so many people's journeys during psychotherapy work.

I'm grateful to those many clients for sharing their struggles to move beyond their troubled worlds, revealing the deepest abuses and fighting so hard to forgive themselves and others. I pray that life has been kinder to them all since our contacts and that they have found some peace.

This book also is rooted in decades of studying and teaching psychotherapy, psychology, counseling, peace studies and sociology. I taught these subjects as an adjunct professor, and although I was poorly paid, that work caused me to develop a great deal of knowledge about human beings, including ethics, gender science, cognitive errors, peacemaking, social movements, child development, and psychodiagnosis. It was an invaluable education beyond my doctorate.

Interpersonal Science & Systems Theory

I have focused on interpersonal science for most of my career, especially from my intensive training in group dynamics, systems and interpersonal studies at the University of Missouri Counseling Psychology doctoral program. I was extremely fortunate to have the guidance of John McGowan, Dennis Kivligan and others during my doctoral studies at University of Missouri for the interpersonal insights and concepts they taught that still underlie most of my work, and shaped me into a scholar and constant learner.

I was also very fortunate to learn about Systems Theory from Richard Caple, a wonderful teacher and mentor during my doctoral studies. Systems thinking has helped me to pull all of these academic threads together and to see relationships as living, constantly changing entities. Systems Theory connects everything to everything for me, and explains the patterns of chaos, change and trauma in life.

Together these shaped me into an interpersonal systems scholar. Gradually I have written up my understanding about these into Interpersonal Systems Theory, which concern the various levels of interpersonal systems (couples, families, communities, nations...). In 2005, I published an article about Group Systems Theory, and later expanded it to the slightly broader Interpersonal Systems Theory.

We

I have consciously used a 'we' voice whenever possible in writing these poems, because I am striving for a wider lens, for interpersonal systems thinking, about how we practice life together. When we do not look at how we create the world together and the major influences we have on each other, we lose some degree of vision and choice in our lives. We must learn to see that we are together, that each of us is not the lone source of meaning in life, and that 'they' are not really separate.

It is not my intention that anyone should ever feel constrained to behave as "we", to give up individual choice in any way. It should be a conscious choice, to behave for me or to behave for us. Couples make that choice several times every day, sometimes consciously, sometimes not. The world might be a better place if all of us thought about each other's welfare more of the time.

If any of you find a serious error in this difficult 'we' form, please write to me and share that information for the betterment of all. I hope that the ideas expressed here merit whatever pain might come from my verbal deviations.

The Road to Love

Most of us like to think we're going somewhere in this life, that life is a journey from infancy to death. Though for many the destination is hazy and complicated, most of us are hoping that we will find love in the end.

If we believe love is the meaning for our journey, we look for signs, teachings or ideals to guide us to the right road to love. But there are many different views of what love is, and some are contradictory, so we have to make many difficult choices.

Some of us wander off the road, or try different roads while others stick with one path. Those of us who wander are often not satisfied with the usual answers and are looking for more complex ways to adapt to the pressures of our lives. These other roads are often hazardous with many wrong turns but we must press on until we find the ways that work for us.

Our way is further complicated by having to balance outer needs (relationships, jobs, community pressures) with the inner goals we are seeking. At the same time, we are coping with various social issues that are also changing, such as the road to justice, the road to respect between people, the road to compassion and the road to peace and all their demands.

My research seems to point to positive relationships, self-love and loving kindness as the choices that work most consistently.

Everyone has to find their own answers to this balancing act.

Gratitude for Spiritual Teachings

Buddhism has taught me so much about love and peace, and has changed my life immensely for the better. Buddhist teachings about loving kindness, equanimity (staying calm during trouble) and maitri (compassion and kindness for oneself) have had a major influence on these poems, so I appreciate the many people who have helped me understand these concepts, especially teachers Pema Chodron, Lama Shenpen Drolma and Thich Nhat Hanh.

Much appreciation is also due to Sufi teachers Deborah Sabura Perry and Sarah Morgan who both influenced and encouraged me as a poet. I'm also grateful to many Sufi friends for sharing the wisdom of the 99 names (expressions) of God, an incredible body of wisdom. The Sufi poetry of Rumi and Hafez were also extremely influential to my understanding and inspiration (If you want to check them out, please look for true translations, not the rearrangements).

I'm also grateful for the many other spiritual teachings that have guided me, including those of Gurdjieff, Emmanuel, Ram Dass, and the Goddess teachings. In addition, I've learned so much about love and peace from the writings of Dr. Martin Luther King, Jr., Mohandas Gandhi, Morihei Ueshiba, Vandana Shiva and Arundhati Roy.

What Else?

Someone once said they loved their writings as if they were their children, and I feel that about these poems as well. Each one carries much toil, care and attachment, and for each I applied some discipline to help them fit into proper company. They also don't get along with each other at times. I cherish them all despite their odd looks and their occasional bad behavior.

When I have left this life, I wish for any benefits or proceeds from my poetry and other writings to go to disadvantaged adolescent and young adult females and queers.

JV Connors, Ph.D.
jvconnors7 at gmail dot com,
Interpersonal Peace Center
Silver City, NM

Acknowledgments

I wish to express deep gratitude to all my life companions who have loved me, supported me and put up with my failings, including family, friends, teachers and coworkers. I especially want to thank my sister, Kathleen Connors for sharing her evocative photographs, many taken near here, to become part of this book.

Much thanks goes to my LGBTQ, Lesbian, Gay, Bi, Trans and Queer friends for welcoming me into their circles, for their generous company, and for tolerating my dumb questions and vegetarianism. I've been very deeply touched by their acceptance.

I also am extremely grateful for my Black, Latino, American Indian, Middle Eastern, Philipino and other friends of color, who have shared their strength, intelligence and vulnerability with me over the years. My life has been greatly enriched by their friendships and knowledge.

Lastly, many thanks to Rick Stansberger being my writing mentor when no one else would take me on, and to poet and friend Mohja Kahf for constantly inspiring me with the magic and power of poetry. I'm also grateful for the poetry of Rainer Maria Rilke, Kahlil Gibran, Wendell Berry, Susan Oliver, Miller Williams and Walt Whitman among many others, which have been a balm to my soul during many difficult times.

Quote References

Brown, Rita Mae (1976). *A plain brown rapper*. Diana Press.

Erdrich, Louise (2005). *The painted drum*. New York: Harper.

Hurston, Zora Neal (1937). *Their eyes were watching God*. Philadelphia: J. B. Lippincott.

May, Rollo (1969). *Love and will*. New York: Norton.

Novalis / Georg Philipp Friedrich Freiherr von Hardenberg (1798). Unsequenced quote https://en.wikiquote.org/wiki/Novalis

Rumi, Maulana Jalal al-Din, translator: Khalili, Nader, (2001). *Rumi: Dancing the flame*. Hesperia, CA: Cal-Earth Press.

Sappho, (630-570 BC). *Sappho, selected poems and fragments.* Poetry in Translation https://www.poetryintranslation.com/PITBR/Greek/Sappho.php#anchor_Toc76357048

Sartre, Jean-Paul (1938). *Nausea.*

Shakespeare, William (1623). *As you like it.* Internet Shakespeare Editions https://internetshakespeare.uvic.ca/Library/Texts/AYL/

Shantideva, translator: Padmakara Translation Group (1997). *Way of the Bodhisattva*. Boston: Shambhala.

 **Author JV Connors** *has a Phd in Counseling Psychology from the University of Missouri, Columbia. She has been a psychotherapist for 40 years and was also an adjunct professor of peace studies, counseling, psychology and sociology for 20 years. She has also been a peace and justice activist and an advocate for wildlife and wilderness.*

*JV. has been writing psychological articles and poetry for 20 years. She is the author of '***Love Catalogue, Book 1: Poems for 101 Varieties of Love***', and is working on 'Love Catalogue, Book 2. She lives in the mountains of New Mexico and can be reached at jvconnors7 at gmail dot com*

 ***Photographer Kathleen Connors*** *lives in Kansas City, Kansas and has been involved in art and photography her entire life. She graduated from the University of Kansas in Lawrence, Kansas with a degree in art education and has since furthered her love of art by studying at the Art Institute of Kansas City, Johnson County Community College in addition to many other workshops and classes. All of the images here are digital photographic images.*

Through her work, she hopes to convey the beauty found in nature and the outside world. She hopes that you enjoy these photographs. Find more on Kathleen Connors' Instagram page **connors.kathleenj**

...We're All Bozos on This Bus

Firesign Theater, title of second album (1971)